RANK ISN'T LEADERSHIP

A Subordinate's Perspective on Policing and Command Failure

C.G. Allen

Rank Isn't Leadership

ISBN: 979-8-90417-365-4

Independently Published

Disclaimer:

This book is based on professional experience and publicly available information. The views expressed are those of the author and do not represent any specific agency, organization, or governing body.

This book is intended for educational and informational purposes only.

First Edition

Dedication

To those who lead without recognition—and those willing to learn the difference.

To my wife and daughters: Through your support and unwavering belief in me, you're the reason this came to fruition. I love you with all my heart and blood.

Acknowledgments

This book reflects my years of experience in law enforcement, including patrol, investigations, supervision, and training. It captures the environments I've worked in and, more importantly, the people I've worked with and for.

Across various assignments and jurisdictions, one constant has remained—the officers on the line. The ones who adapt quickly, make decisions under pressure, and carry responsibility whether leadership is present or not.

Their actions, consistency, and perspective shaped this book. I've worked with leaders who set standards through presence, clarity, and accountability. I've also seen the consequences when those qualities are missing. Both experiences matter and are reflected here.

 To those who trained me, challenged me, and trusted me then and now, your influence is evident in my approach to this profession and my view of leadership within it.

To the officers still doing this job every day—handling uncertainty, making decisions with limited information, and standing firm when it matters—this perspective comes from that shared reality.

To my family, your support made this possible. You've carried the weight of this profession in ways that I can't put into words, and that means more than anything written here.

Preface

This book is not written to be comfortable. It is written to be accurate. Law enforcement leadership is often discussed in theory, but must be experienced in reality. This book reflects that reality, from the line where decisions are carried out, and consequences are lived through in real time.

It is time to change the mindset and focus on developing leaders. Leaders will help maintain retention and bring back a positive reputation to modern policing.

Contents

Author Bio

C.G. Allen is a law enforcement professional with nearly two decades of experience in patrol, investigations, supervision, and training. Having served in multiple jurisdictions, Allen brings a frontline perspective to leadership, focusing on the gap between policy and real-world application.

His work centers on leadership under pressure, officer development, and the operational realities that shape decision-making in modern policing.

Introduction: The Sound of Silence

This book isn't theory. I've lived it, and I'm still living it.

I've been at scenes where everything appears to be working. Units respond, lights flash, radios are active. From the outside, it looks controlled. But on the inside, it's anything but that.

There's a moment that happens in this job. It doesn't come at the start of a shift or when things are busy. It occurs when things slow down, when the end of the shift is near.

Usually late, somewhere between 3:00 and 5:00 AM. The radio goes quiet, calls are cleared, and reports are finished. Then, out of nowhere, something doesn't feel right. I've been doing this long enough to recognize that something is coming. You check your radio. Then you check it again. Not because you need to, but because you want to make sure it still works, since the silence was deafening.

Then it appears on the computer. An address and a vague description of the call. Then the radio keys up for the call to come out. Incomplete information that's rushed and unclear. Officers acknowledge, and questions start immediately. Guaranteed someone is already moving before the details are finished.

Then the tone changes. Not officially and not through dispatch. But everyone hears it. More units respond, and radio traffic overlaps as information comes in pieces.

Someone arrives on the scene and gives an update that tells you everything you need to know. It's not a *routine call.*

And then it happens.

Silence.

Rank Isn't Leadership

It is not the absence of radio traffic. It's something else. It can be heard clearly—in hesitation, in the gaps between transmissions. In the way people start waiting, not for permission but for direction.

I've stood on scenes where supervisors were present. Rank is there, but no one was taking control. To an outsider, it looked functional. From the inside, it was fragmented. Officers started making decisions on their own, not because they wanted to, but because they had to.

That's when you understand something that doesn't show up in reports.

Something that isn't taught in training. Something that isn't measured in promotions.

Rank is present.

Leadership is not.

This book exists because of that moment and similar ones. Because it's not just a single moment; it's a pattern that repeats. Across calls, across shifts, across agencies. The same breakdown. The same silence.

Leadership in law enforcement is always a topic of discussion. It's covered in classrooms, policies, and promotion processes. But true leadership isn't proven there. It's demonstrated when information is incomplete, circumstances are changing, and hesitation creates risk. That's when leadership either emerges or it doesn't.

This isn't written from the top down. It's written from the line, where decisions are made in seconds, and consequences are immediate. Where leadership is not theoretical, it's visible.

This is not about criticizing individuals. It's about identifying a pattern—a gap between rank and leadership—that affects decision-making, trust, performance, and retention. If you've done this job long enough, you've seen it, felt it, and adapted to it.

Because work doesn't stop when leadership is absent, someone always steps up—it's just not always the person with the rank. This book explores that gap, where it exists, why it exists, and what happens when it's ignored. In this profession, when things go wrong, there's no time to debate leadership. You either have it— or you don't.

PART I: THE REALITY ON THE LINE

Chapter 1: The Disconnect No One Fixes

There's a gap in law enforcement that doesn't show up in reports, audits, or performance metrics. Command staff doesn't see what we see. Not because Command staff doesn't care—but because it can't be seen from that position. The view is filtered. It comes through reports, briefings, and data—clear, structured, and arranged to imply control. By the time information reaches the top, it has already been interpreted and condensed, and it lacks full context. I've been on the other side—where none of that shows what's really happening.

 To some extent, it's understandable. Command staff no longer work in the trenches; the view of modern policing comes only from reports or occasional glimpses of body camera footage when there is reason to review it for potential litigation or policy violations.

What command sees:

- Clean reports
- Structured briefings
- Metrics that suggest control

What the line experiences:

- Calls with incomplete information
- Situations changing in real time
- Decisions made without direction
- Accountability applied after the fact, without context

- Decisions made in isolation

- After-action scrutiny without considering context

- Damnation for split-second decisions and no recognition for successes

- Promotions or recognition of achievements based on nepotism

- Denied training requests and mentorship

There is a gap between these two realities, and that gap is where leadership fails. That gap isn't just theoretical; it's operational. It's where leadership starts to break down. We avoid discussing it in meetings but talk about it after shifts — in patrol cars and between calls. These conversations are consistent, regardless of the agency.

- "They weren't there."

- "They don't get it."

- "We're on our own."

This isn't insubordination but adaptation. Because the work doesn't stop just because leadership is absent. Someone always steps up; it's just not always the person wearing the rank.

Chapter 2: If It Makes Sense, We Don't Do It.

I've heard it countless times and have even said it: "If it makes sense, we don't do it." It's not a joke; it's learned behavior. It reflects how decisions are made. Over time, we learn something that isn't taught in any academy or policy manual. It's the result of watching good ideas get shut down repeatedly until people stop trying.

It shows that logic does not guide decision-making. That efficiency is often sacrificed for tradition, and common sense is frequently overridden by bureaucracy and nepotism. Logic doesn't always drive outcomes, but process does.

When a process consistently overrides logic, behavior changes. In law enforcement, we talk a lot about discretion, judgment, and experience. We say we trust our people to make decisions in dynamic situations. But then a system is built that quietly punishes those same decisions if they fall outside the safest, most defensible interpretation of policy.

So what happens?

We stop asking, "What makes sense?"
We start asking, "What keeps me out of trouble?"

I have seen this happen on calls for service more times than I can count.

Destiny

Rank Isn't Leadership

There is an address I recognize before the dispatcher even finishes saying it. It meant one thing, Destiny.

Destiny became a recurring call—drug addiction, mental health, escalating violence. One call changed everything.

Destiny, at the time, was in her mid-twenties. She lived with her grandmother, who had been trying to manage a situation she was never equipped for. Every call was a version of the same cycle until it was not.

Dispatch came over the radio with panic in the background. Not frustration—panic. When I arrived, I was alone. Backup was still on its way. The house smelled just like it always did—lavender, baked goods, that familiar, old scent that did not match what was happening inside. Her grandmother was bleeding badly.

The scene is unstable, and Destiny is nowhere in sight. The decision had to be made immediately. There was no time for policy debates. I could not have even told you what policy would dictate at that moment; only action was needed. This is where leadership matters: in real time, under pressure, without perfect information, and with no hindsight.

Blood poured out of Destiny's grandmother's head. One thing I learned over the years is that head wounds do not have to look serious to be serious, and this one was. Blood was everywhere. Her grandmother was disoriented, scared, and in denial about what happened. I asked where Destiny had gone, and all she could say was "She ran."

As I checked the home for anyone else inside, I found the weapon —
a heavy glass ashtray. The old heavy style from the seventies.
Squared, dark ember colored glass, caked with decades of cigarettes
and now with blood and hair. I went back to my car to grab my med
kit and advised dispatch to stage EMS. Backup is still on the way.
When I came back to the door, there Destiny was, blocking my way
to her grandmother and standing at the base of the stairs.

Destiny's hands were covered in blood, and now she was holding a
large piece of rusted metal. No yelling, no movement, just staring
directly at me. I gave commands—calm, direct, clear. She did not
respond like she usually would to me; then she charged.

I deployed my taser, and to my surprise, it made full contact. Destiny
dropped immediately, hitting the ground hard and breaking her nose
on impact.

Now even more blood-soaked, I secured her, placed her in the patrol
car, and went back to render aid. The situation was under control. The
grandmother was taken to the hospital and survived. Destiny was also
taken to the hospital and then to the county jail. By every operational
standard, the outcome was correct. That is not where the evaluation
took place; it happened afterward.

After the Call

Comments. Jokes. Questions that were not really questions, like, "How come I was scared of a little girl?" Why use the Taser? Why not go hands-on? Why not handle it differently? At one point, I was directly told I should have fought her instead and taken the opportunity to punch her in the face. That moment matters more than the call itself because that is where the lesson gets learned.

Not the official lesson — the real one. The one we carry with us to the next call. I realized I can make the right choice. However, I can still be second-guessed, because it did not meet expectations.

It did not matter that I had dealt with Destiny countless times before. Alternatively, that I had seen her strength after a day or night of binging on various substances, or the insane strength she had when extremely irate and high, I would still be second-guessed because what my leadership thought I could do did not align with what I should do.

This is the kind of leadership that's currently mentoring young officers. The situation becomes unnecessarily complicated because logic has been abandoned, leaving only emotion. Our disdain for dealing with Destiny so often would have caused a less experienced officer to act on emotion, which could have cost lives.

When I respond to a call for service, the process is not complicated. I arrive, assess the situation, and within seconds, I know what needs to be done. It's simple. It's not risky. It is just common sense, backed by experience. However, then something else sneaks in.

- Policy
- Liability
- Second-guessing
- Command staff who were not there will read the report later with the benefit of hindsight.

So instead of acting decisively, people hesitate. Supervisors or poorly lead subordinates get caught in the cycle. Things get slowed down when action needs to take place. Things get sped up when taking a few moments would change the outcome. Calls for unnecessary resources are made just to spread the responsibility around. Not because it helps the situation—but because it provides a false sense of protection from liability.

That is where the phrase lives. "If it makes sense, we don't do it."

It is not about incompetence; it is about conditioning. We create the problems we are trying to avoid when we think emotionally rather than logically. It would have made sense to handle it, but we did not. The system does not reward outcomes. It rewards compliance.

I can solve a problem quickly, cleanly, and professionally—but if I step outside the expected process, even for the right reasons, I take on risk. Not the kind of risk we train for on the street, but administrative risk. Career risk.

So over time, we adapt, and it is done by:

- No longer being proactive
- No longer using discretion unless it is safe

- Working inside the lines of policy, even when the lines do not fit the situation

Moreover, that is where the gap forms—the one that can be felt but not always articulated. From the outside, everything looks functional. Calls are handled, reports are written, and the shift ends. Do it all again tomorrow. We are not always doing what works, but what survives review.

"If it makes sense, we don't do it." It reflects a system that claims it seeks leadership, judgment, and initiative—but quietly discourages them. Moreover, the longer we remain in this role, the more it becomes clear that the hardest part is not always making the calls. It is navigating the space between what we know is right… and what we are allowed to do.

Where the Mindset Comes From

This mindset does not come out of nowhere. It stems from repeated experiences where logical solutions are ignored, delayed, or replaced with more complex ones.

Early in my career, I was assigned to the violent offender unit in the county jail. Four dorms with over a hundred inmates in each. Every day involves physical altercations, cell extractions, and constant tension.

The problem was not the inmates; it was the inconsistency. Rules were enforced differently depending on the officer, the day the officer was having, and other factors. Expectations changed without warning. Discipline lacked structure. That inconsistency created more conflict on top of what was already there.

So, I built a solution and a simple one at that. I took the phrase from the corrections academy, *"Fair, Firm, Consistent"*.

A simple phrase, but a good foundation. I wrote standardized expectations for both inmates and officers. A clear procedure with a script for officers to use before recreation began.

Fair. Firm. Consistent.

I had a lieutenant who wanted to test it. We started small, implementing it only on our shift at first. The results were immediate and better than we thought. Even the inmates had less to complain about.

There were fewer physical altercations, better control of the housing unit, and improved efficiency, allowing us actually to leave on time at the end of the shift.

When I presented the idea to the command staff, it was quickly dismissed without any discussion. Immediate responses indicated that the process was not broken and did not need fixing.

Over the next year, the command staff changed twice. I submitted the proposal again, and it was denied again. Finally, a new command staff was brought in after an election. I submitted it one more time; it was approved and is still in place today.

The Lesson That Actually Gets Learned

This is how the mindset forms: not from policy but from experience—both good and bad.

An officer finds a quicker way to handle a recurring problem. It is safer, faster, and more practical. But it gets shut down. Just like what happened to me. It gets denied not because it is wrong, but because:

- "That is not how we have done it."

- "Policy does not say that."

- "That would require approval."

- "We tried something like that before."

- Or the unspoken response that it was not the idea of command.

Over time, the lesson becomes clear. Not the lesson leadership intended to provide, but the one we take from it.

Logic Is Secondary to The System.

What That Does to an Organization

When that belief takes hold, something predictable happens. We stop offering solutions, pushing ideas, or stop trying. Not because we lack motivation, it is there, or it was. It is because there is no return on it.

The result means initiative declines, innovation disappears, effort becomes minimal, and compliance replaces thinking. This is not laziness. It is an adaptation of self-preservation. Because from the line, the message is clear:

Thinking creates resistance.

Compliance avoids it.

The Organizational Cost

When logic is consistently dismissed, agencies do not just lose efficiency. Something far more precious is lost. People. Officers begin to do only what is required. We avoid suggesting improvements and prioritize self-protection over problem-solving.

Over time, the organization becomes slower to adapt and operates less effectively. The entire organization becomes reactive and not proactive, at least in practice. In policy, the organization will state that part of its mission is to provide a proactive approach to policing for the community. Furthering the increasingly disconnect from reality.

All of this leads to one outcome: it eventually becomes a place people no longer want to work.

The Leadership Failure Behind It

This is not a line-level issue but purely a leadership failure.

Specifically, a failure to distinguish the difference between control and effectiveness. The ability to distinguish the process from the outcome. Or worse, confusing tradition with purpose.

Leaders who rely strictly on rigid processes believe they are maintaining order. What those same leaders are actually creating is stagnation.

This is frustrating and confusing because policing is not static. Call types change in an instant. Threats evolve rapidly, and the communities will shift just as fast. Leadership must evolve with these changes.

Historical Leaders Who Rejected This Thinking

Abraham Lincoln was known for surrounding himself with individuals who disagreed with him. He did not suppress dissent—he used it. He listened to competing ideas, evaluated them, and made decisions based on what worked, not what was traditional. (Phillips, 1992).

Lincoln understood something critical:

Good ideas are not rank-dependent. (Phillips, 1992) Read it again! *Good ideas are not rank-dependent*! In law enforcement, that matters because the best idea at the moment may come from the newest officer on the scene, not the highest-ranking one.

Theodore Roosevelt approached leadership with a mix of discipline and adaptability. His philosophy—often summarized as "speak softly and carry a big stick"—was not about rigidity. It emphasized controlled strength combined with practical, logical action. Roosevelt believed in taking action rather than hesitating, & prioritizing practicality over paralysis. He did not wait for perfect conditions; instead, he acted based on what made sense at the moment.

That mindset directly applies to policing. Waiting for perfect policy alignment in a dynamic situation often causes delays.

Winston Churchill led Britain through one of its most uncertain times. His leadership was not characterized by strict adherence to tradition— it was defined by adaptability under pressure. Churchill made decisions with incomplete information and constantly adjusted his strategy in response to changing circumstances. He communicated clearly, acted decisively, and understood that survival relied on flexibility—not bureaucracy. (Hayward) He did not ask, "Is this how it's always been done?"

He asked, "Will this work right now?" (Hayward)
Need an example? The Ministry of Ungentlemanly Warfare. This was a completely outside-the-box idea that created a legendary unit responsible for delivering true destruction to the Axis forces and made for a great movie, thank you, Guy Ritchie!

The Policing Reality: Where Logic Gets Lost

In law enforcement, the rejection of logical solutions often comes from three places:

1. Overreliance on Policy

Policy is necessary. It provides structure, consistency, and some legal protection. But policy is not designed to account for every real-world variable; it is not possible to.

When leaders treat policy as the ceiling instead of the foundation, decision-making stops. Policies should guide critical thinking, not replace it. In dynamic situations, critical thinking is what saves lives. I've never seen a life saved because of perfect policy alignment. Policy should inform action, not replace thinking. How many training sessions have you attended where complacency kills? Policy can't replace free critical thinking.

2. Fear-Based Decision Making

Leaders sometimes reject logical solutions not because of being flawed, but because of uncertainty.

"What if it goes wrong?"
"What if we get questioned?"
"What if this becomes an issue later?"

So instead, leaders rely on what is known—even if it's inefficient. This is not leadership; it's risk avoidance and cowardice. In a profession centered on managing risk, avoiding it entirely isn't an option.

The Subordinate Perspective on Logic

Observation of this pattern of behavior is clear. We, as officers, identify problems, develop solutions, and informally test ideas, then watch what happens when those ideas reach leadership. If we are ignored, dismissed, or things become too complicated, a shift occurs.

You start to hear:

- "Just do it the way they want."

- "Don't overthink it."

- "It's not worth the headache."

- "It is what it is."

That isn't compliance. That's disengagement, and once that mindset takes hold, it spreads.

Rebuilding a Culture That Values Thinking

If an agency wants to eliminate the "if it makes sense, we don't do it" mindset, leadership must actively work to reverse it.

1. Reward Practical Solutions

When officers identify effective improvements, leaders must recognize and implement them when appropriate. Not just symbolically, but operationally. Public acknowledgment and praise within the organization should also follow. Providing feedback to us that suggestions are not only accepted but also reviewed.

2. Encourage Questioning Without Punishment

Questioning the system isn't insubordination; it's engagement. Leaders who suppress it only create silence. Leaders who listen foster progress. If subordinates perform well, it reflects on the leader. It shows cultivation and mentorship.

3. Train Decision-Making, Not Just Compliance

We need training to think, not just follow orders. Because in real-world situations, thinking is what keeps people alive.

4. Lead with Intent, Not Just Instruction

Clear intent provides flexibility. Rigid instructions restrict it. When we understand the "why," we can modify the "how."

The Reality Leaders Must Accept

The phrase "if it makes sense, we don't do it" is more than sarcasm; it is feedback. It reflects how leadership decisions are perceived at the operational level. Whether leaders recognize it or not, it influences behavior because we will always adapt to the environment leadership creates.

Final Truth

Law enforcement remains a noble profession. It relies on judgment— making rapid decisions with limited information and high stakes. If logic isn't permitted in that environment, then leadership has already fallen short.

Because in the moments that matter most, there will be no time for:

- Approval chains

- Perfect policy alignment

- Bureaucratic process

There will only be one question: *What makes sense right now?*

The agencies that empower their people to respond accurately, confidently, and with support are the ones that will succeed. The rest will keep saying, "If it makes sense, we don't do it." Get ready because they will never understand why nothing improves.

PART II: BREAKING THE ILLUSION

Chapter 3: The Lie about Rank

A promotion should carry meaning—an achievement, an honor. It is designed to signal competence, readiness, trust, and the ability to lead during tough times. On paper, it does. However, in practice, that assumption does not last long.

It does not take months to see the difference. Sometimes it takes one shift, and in some cases, just one call for service. We do not need evaluations or formal reviews to recognize it. We see in real time who steps up and who hesitates. We see who takes control and who runs away from it.

That judgment is immediate, and once it is made, it does not go away. It has become a lasting impression.

What Rank Actually Does

Rank creates structure, and it defines authority and responsibility. However, structure is not leadership. Leadership shows up when structure starts to break down. When information is incomplete, when conditions change, and when hesitation creates risk.

That is where the true distinction is made.

How We Promote

Most promotional systems rely on measurable criteria such as written exams, policy knowledge, time in service, and administrative performance. All these things matter; they are not trivial, but none of them guarantee leadership.

Written exams will measure memory recall. Oral boards measure controlled responses. Scenario testing simulates decision-making—but removes the variables that matter most:

- Time pressure

- Uncertainty

- Human unpredictability

- Consequences

Without those elements, the system evaluates performance under ideal conditions. It leaves out the reality of unpredictable behavior and the consequences that follow.

What That Produces

The outcome is predictable. Supervisors who understand policy—but struggle to apply it in real time. Leaders who can manage structure—but cannot command a scene in the moment.

That gap is not theoretical. It shows up as hesitation, unclear directions, and a lack of control under pressure.

The Illusion of Fairness

Standardized testing creates the appearance of fairness. It is objective, measurable, and defensible. However, fairness does not equal effectiveness. Why?

Because the system prioritizes what can be measured and ignores what actually matters. Maintaining that command presence, executing decision-making under pressure, having clarity in chaos, and ownership of the outcome.

Qualities that are harder to quantify and, as a result, are often overlooked. However, what happens when they are overlooked? The result is consistent; the wrong people end up in the right positions.

The Operational Consequence

When rank and leadership do not align, everyone's behavior changes. Officers will follow directions when they are given. However, we do not always rely on it. Instead, we will operate laterally, trust our experience over instructions, and depend on each other rather than on leadership.

To be clear, that is not a form of rebellion. It is an adaptation because the job still has to get done.

What Meaningful Change Looks Like

Contrary to popular belief, changes can be made without requiring additional budget requests or abandoning the current structure. It requires redefining what matters.

A strong system would evaluate:

- Decisions made while dealing with pressure, not just what the policy said.
- Demonstrate the ability to take control of the scene, not just talk about it like in a classroom setting.
- Communication clarity, not adding to the confusion by making things clear and concise.
- Accountability, including how the candidate handles failure.

The Bottom Line

Promotion systems are not broken because they test knowledge. That is not what is broken. The promotional systems are broken because they stop there at knowledge. They do not measure the behaviors, decisions, and actions that happen when things go wrong. Until they do, the gap will remain. To us on the line, that gap is always obvious.

Chapter 4: Management vs Leadership- Authority vs Influence

The difference between management and leadership is not learned in a classroom or during a training session. It becomes clear on a call for service. A call that starts routine, then, out of nowhere, changes.

Information shifts quickly, and conditions evolve into something far more. Officers arrive, and the cogs of the machine begin moving, but not together or in coordination, like a watch put back together incorrectly. It is moving, but just not like how it should.

Then a supervisor arrives. For a moment, everything pauses. Hopes of fine-tuning to make everything run smoother. Then the order comes, "Handle it."

That is management, not leadership.

Authority vs Influence

Management relies on authority while leadership relies on influence. Authority can force action, but influence creates commitment. That difference is not philosophical; it is operational.

The Flowchart Problem

Management is like a step-by-step style interpretation of leadership. Management often follows a predictable pattern:

If X happens → do Y
If Y fails → do Z

It works in controlled environments, such as a classroom. It fails in real-world situations because they do not follow flowcharts.

They change, and when they change, people need to think critically and fast. That is where management reaches its limit.

What Leadership Actually Provides

Leadership does not eliminate uncertainty; it prepares people to operate within it. It offers clarity of purpose. The understanding of intent regarding the mission at hand. The confidence to act even when guidance is not immediately clear or available.

That is what allows a team to keep going when the initial plan falls apart. When plans break down—and believe me, they will—those are the elements that keep operations moving.

What the Line Evaluates

Leadership is not judged during routine calls; nevertheless, when we see how that person handles the information, it is incomplete, and a decision must be made with the risk of real consequences.

In those moments, we are watching three things: Presence, Clarity, and Accountability.

Management can exist without those things, but leadership cannot.

What Happens When Leadership Is Missing

The system does not stop; it cannot, it has to adapt. So, officers have ended up becoming less proactive and more cautious. Attention is focused more on avoiding mistakes. Not because we lack ability but because we lack support. So, the more we insulate ourselves, the better the protection we have.

The Difference That Defines Trust

Management will ask: "Was policy followed?"

Leadership asks: "Did we support the decision?"

That ideological difference builds trust, and trust drives performance.

What History Already Proved

The idea that systems should never be questioned has never been a hallmark of effective leadership. In fact, history shows the opposite. Abraham Lincoln understood this long before modern leadership theories emerged. In *Lincoln on Leadership,* Lincoln is shown as a leader who did not rely solely on his official authority.

By surrounding himself with opposing viewpoints, he made decisions under uncertainty and took responsibility for the outcome — even when those decisions failed. Lincoln did not just oversee the Civil War; he led it through action and presence. (Phillips, 1992).

Lincoln made decisions under severe scrutiny, took responsibility for the outcomes, and maintained trust—even as the situation worsened.

Contrast that with what management often looks like in today's law enforcement setting.

Chapter 5: Rank Does Not Equal Leadership-Authority Assigned, Trust Earned

There is a simple truth in this profession that is not said often enough: *Rank is assigned, and leadership is earned.*

Furthermore, the two do not always align.

What Actually Drives That Reality

Officers can handle the job and what comes with it—the risks, the workload, the pressure- it is expected. I will not say it was known when we started, but there was an understanding that it would be present.

What wears us down is not the public. It is inconsistency and absence of leadership, and/or leadership that does not match the responsibility that comes with it.

That is what affects morale and drives people away.

How Leadership Is Measured

I have never seen leadership evaluated in formal settings. I wish we did, and it could be an open discussion. However, it is evaluated through patterns observed by officers.

What we look for is simple: What do you do when it matters? Do you take control as a leader? Do you hesitate? Do you commit to decisions? Most importantly, do you avoid responsibility?

Those answers define leadership, not the rank assigned.

Management vs Leadership in Practice

Management will ensure that calls are assigned, reports are completed in full, and policies are followed.

It is important because it maintains structure and keeps the system functioning. However, it does not build trust.

Without trust, performance drops to the minimum required to avoid problems. It does not put performance at the level required to solve problems.

The Second Leadership Structure

Every agency has two chains of command: The official one and the real one.

The official chain is based on rank assigned or achieved. The real chain is based on trust and influence. It is made up of the people everyone turns to when things start to go wrong.

The ones who step in without being told and make decisions confidently or stabilize situations before directions are given.

They do not always hold rank, but they hold the influence the formal leaders need. When conditions become unpredictable—

People follow influence.

The Organizational Problem

Leadership often sees this informal leader as a threat. It is not. It is a symptom. When informal leadership replaces formal leadership, the issue is not the people stepping up. It is the absence of those who should be.

What Officers Actually Want

We are not asking for perfection; we know it is not possible. What we expect is simple. We need guidance amid uncertainty, presence and participation during difficult moments, and, above all, accountability when things go wrong.

When those exist, performance improves, and not because the job gets easier. Because leadership is doing its job. James Mattis underscores this in *Call Sign Chaos*. Mattis repeatedly emphasizes that leadership involves making decisions in uncertain situations and accepting the responsibility that comes with it. He highlights the importance of clarity of purpose rather than just issuing orders. He did not simply tell Marines what to do. (Mattis & West, 2019) He ensured their understanding of:

- The mission
- The purpose
- The commander's intent

So that when the plan inevitably goes off-script, decisive action can still be made. That is the key difference. Management depends on control, while leadership prepares people to operate when control is lost and to regain it through critical thinking, logic, and reasoning grounded in a solid understanding of policy.

In policing, control is often temporary and an illusion at best. Calls change, information updates, and situations escalate. An officer's skills and experience vary from one officer to another. No supervisor can predict every outcome, and trying to do so would waste time. So, the real question becomes: What happens when the plan collapses?

There are two different reactions. Management encounters obstacles and often hesitates, while leaders act. From the subordinate perspective, this is where the evaluation of the leader occurs. This distinction is where many law enforcement organizations unintentionally promote managers rather than leaders.

The Defining Question

When things go wrong, who takes control? If that answer is unclear, the issue is not management. It is the absence of leadership.

There is a simple truth in this profession that is not said often enough: rank is assigned, but leadership is earned. Moreover, the two do not always align.

Chapter 6: Trust — What Gets Broken Doesn't Reset

My father never talked about his time in the Army. Not in the way most people would expect. Not in any detail. There were limited stories of just humorous events.

After he died unexpectedly at 51, I started asking questions. At his funeral, hundreds of people showed up. Men I had never met who carried themselves differently from the average person present. They were quiet and controlled, not because of mourning. That is when I realized there was more to his story than he ever said.

I filed a Freedom of Information Act request for his military records. What I received back was a file filled with blacked-out lines and redacted and incomplete.

I remember when I asked him about his service before he passed, his answer never changed: "It was work." That was it. However, I did not need details to understand what it did to him. I saw it in the way he carried himself and the way he made decisions. But I also saw how people responded to him.

I did discover he had been a U.S. Army Ranger, and whatever that experience built in him, it wasn't loud. It was controlled and undeniable. People followed him. Not because they had to, but because they trusted him.

Subordinates didn't question him, but he wasn't above approach.

Leadership didn't interfere with him because there was an understanding that didn't need to be explained: Whatever he was doing, it worked.

The Lesson

As a teenager, I was the opposite of everything he represented. I pushed boundaries. I made bad choices. I hung out with the wrong crowd. And I lied. Not about major, life-changing things. The kind of things teenagers lie about for no real reason other than convenience or to avoid getting in trouble, and not realizing the lie was worse than the act committed. Nevertheless, I did it enough so that it stopped feeling normal. It turned into a pattern, and patterns test patience.

One day, after another lie, my father did not argue. He did not lecture. He did not raise his voice; he rarely did, and that was more terrifying. He sent me to the backyard. My instructions were simple: "dig a hole. Four feet wide, four feet long, and four feet deep. And do not mess up the sod."

It was summer in Chicago: hot, humid, heavy air that does not move. I dug. At first, I thought it was just punishment. Something physical. Something meant to wear me down, and it did. Nevertheless, I pushed through it and finished the hole. I went to him and told him I was done.

He came, looked at the hole without emotion, then gave me the next instruction, simply saying, "Fill it back in."

Once it was filled and the sod was placed back as gently as possible, I called for him again. He looked at the ground, then looked at me and asked, "Where is my hole?" That went on for two days. Dig. Fill. Dig again. Four holes. Four separate times. No explanation. No discussion. Just work.

When it was over, I expected it to be finished. Punishment served. Lesson learned—whatever it was supposed to teach. That is when he finally explained it. He told me each hole represented someone I had lied to.

One for him, one for my mother, one for my sister, and one for myself because he knew that I was lying to myself about who I was. He said the holes were not the punishment. They were the example. You can fill a hole. You can put the dirt back. Pack it down. Try to make it look like it was never there. Nevertheless, it does not go back the same. The ground is disturbed. The surface looks different. Furthermore, even if you fix it—even if you do everything right to repair it—it takes time for it to

settle—to blend back into being less obvious. Sometimes it never fully does. That is what trust looks like.

From that point on, the lesson stuck—not because of what he said, but because of what I had to do to understand it. I still hate digging holes. However, trust is not about the moment it is broken; it is an important part, but not as critical as everything that comes after, the scars it leaves.

What That Means Here

That lesson directly relates to law enforcement—more than most are willing to admit. Trust is not built through policy. It is not built through speeches, mission statements, or command briefings. It is built in moments. Small ones. Repeated ones. Furthermore, once it is broken, it cannot be reset.

A supervisor fails to support an officer's good decision. That is a hole. A leader disappears when things go wrong. That is a hole. Discipline is enforced inconsistently—another hole. Command questions decisions publicly but stays silent privately—another hole. Each one can be explained and justified. Each one can even be "fixed." However, none of them disappear immediately.

How Officers Track It

I have seen officers track it the same way I tracked those holes — by memory, pattern, and repetition, by the marks left behind. You can rebuild trust, but you do not do it just by saying the right things; you rebuild it through actions.

The Reality Leaders Avoid

Over time, consistently and without expecting immediate results, there is a reality most leaders do not want to accept: some holes do not fully disappear. As a leader, that becomes part of your legacy. Not just what you did right, but what you failed to do.

Leadership often assumes that trust is flexible and can be repaired quickly. That one good decision cancels out a bad one.

It doesn't. From the line, trust is cumulative, but so is damage. And damage is remembered longer than performance.

There are excuses, and there are reasons. Reasons are explanations for poor action or inaction caused by circumstances outside your control. Excuses are explanations for poor action or inaction caused by circumstances within your control. So next time an explanation is given as to why a mission wasn't accomplished, ask yourself: was it a reason or an excuse?

The Bottom Line

When things inevitably go wrong, officers don't rely on policy.

We rely on people. We rely on those who have shown up before when needed and help share the responsibility. And we take note of those who did not.

That is what defines leadership. Not rank, not position, and not authority. Just trust. Once it's broken, you don't reset it, you have to rebuild it.

PART III: THE LEADERSHIP CRISIS

Chapter 7: The Leadership Crisis in Modern Policing

If everything in this book feels familiar, it is because it is not unique. This is not specific to one agency and not one experience. It is widespread, and it has been measured. The gap between rank and leadership is an operational gap. That gap is driving one of the most critical issues in modern policing: Retention.

What Agencies Think the Problem Is

For years, the assumption has been that no one wants to do this job anymore because of the pay, the hours, the workload, or public perception. Those do matter, and it is part of the problem.

Nevertheless, they are not the primary cause.

What the Data Shows

Research consistently points to one factor above all others: Leadership.

It is not the compensation, the workload, or the hours. It's leadership. It aligns with what we see every day. It wears us down constantly, with that absence of leadership and that us-versus-command-staff mentality.

When leadership fails to match responsibility, the realization is:

The public is easier to deal with than your own command staff.

When that realization happens, everything about this job and the way we react to it and how we perform in it changes.

What This Actually Impacts

Leadership determines whether officers stay and the type of performance they deliver while at the agency. Leadership is also the success or failure of the office's trust in the system. Rank tells us who is in charge, but leadership determines whether anyone follows.

This is not New — It has Been Proven for Generations.

This problem did not start in modern policing. Military leadership has wrestled with it for decades.

Chesty Puller did not gain the trust of Marines because of his rank. He earned it through presence, decisiveness, and shared risk. He was visible. He was engaged. He never asked anyone to do something he would not do himself. That is why people followed him. (USAF, 2015)

James Mattis emphasized the same principle years later. Leadership, in its simplest form, is about providing clarity amid chaos. Not control. Not micromanagement. Clarity (Mattis & West, 2019).

The Modern Reality

Policing is no longer what it was even ten years ago.

It operates at the intersection of public scrutiny, staffing shortages, advancing technology, and constant evaluation. We are no longer just responding to crime but to a multifaceted set of sociological issues.

We are operating under continuous observation, and that environment increases pressure. Without strong leadership performance, it does not just decline; it collapses.

The Retention Truth

Officers are not leaving the profession because they cannot do the job. They are leaving because of the environment surrounding them. The consistent issues of burnout, lack of support, constant pressure, and limited professional development. All of those are the symptoms of the underlying cause of leadership.

There is a phrase repeated across professions: "People do not quit jobs. They quit their supervisors." In law enforcement, that is not a cliché. It is a pattern.

The Bottom Line

Modern policing is not at a breaking point because of external pressure. It is at a turning point because of leadership and antiquated ideology surrounding it.

The agencies that succeed will not be the ones with the most resources or the biggest budgets. The agencies that will be successful are those with leaders who provide that missing clarity under pressure. Moreover, they remain consistent under scrutiny; adapt to change and earn trust through their actions.

Because without trust—

Nothing works.

The Leadership Gap

The traditional leadership model in law enforcement is no longer sufficient. Rank-based, command-driven, compliance-focused; it worked in a different time and different environment. It does not work now. Modern leadership requires operating in three domains simultaneously:

1. Internal Leadership (People)

Morale, development, wellness. "Figure it out" supervision no longer works.

2. External Leadership (Community)

Leadership now exists in public view—transparency and perception matter.

3. Adaptive Leadership (Change)

Technology, policy, and society are changing rapidly. Leaders must adapt, not resist.

Failure in any one of these areas creates friction—failure in any one of the three leads to collapse.

Emerging Challenges Leaders Cannot Ignore

The profession is being reshaped in real time.

- Information warfare
  False narratives, viral clips, and misinformation create real-world consequences. (Dr. Joseph J. Lestrange, 2024).

- Workforce evolution
  Civilian roles are expanding. Identity and culture are shifting.

- Trust deficit
  Public trust must now be actively earned, not assumed.
  (Hope, 2020)

Leadership is no longer confined to internal operations. It is constantly being evaluated — both inside and outside the agency.

What Actually Fixes It

The problems are complex. The solution is not. It's leadership. Not just theoretical or positional leadership, but operational leadership. Agencies that stabilize do a few things consistently:

- Build ownership instead of survival.
- Invest in retention, not just recruitment.
- Prioritize wellness without lowering standards.
- Develop front-line supervisors relentlessly.
- Use transparency as a tool, not a liability.
- Make data-driven decisions instead of relying on tradition (Wilson & Weiss, 2012; PERF, 2023).

And most importantly:

Understand that leadership is behavior — not a title.

The Bottom Line

- Modern policing is at a turning point. Not because of the public, politics, or staffing, but because of leadership. The agencies that will succeed are not the ones with the most resources; they are the ones with leaders who:

- Provide clarity under pressure

- Stay consistent under scrutiny

- Adapt without losing their identity

- And earn trust through action

Because at the end of the day, nothing in this profession works without trust. Not policy, rank, or structure. Just people and whether we choose to follow.

Chapter 8: A Different Magic Chair

There is a book every cop has read or should read. *Emotional Survival for Law Enforcement* by Dr. Kevin Gilmartin. In his well-written book, he talked about the use of a magic chair. For those who have not read the book, the Magic Chair refers to an officer coming home and experiencing the adrenaline dump from the day.

Going from a state of hyper-vigilance to a state of depression. An officer will sit in their specific chair at home, become emotionally detached from family, loved ones, and things they once enjoyed, and become isolated. Dr. Gilmartin goes on to describe how to break this cycle by engaging in personal life and hobbies and seeking social interactions with people outside law enforcement to avoid the "fatal" downward spiral. (Ph.D, 2002).

Excellent advice for both new and veteran officers. We need emotional support and sometimes the realization to get out of a rut.

The Moment Everything Changed

I thought I understood leadership before I ever got promoted. I knew the job and my agency's policy. I handled calls, made decisions, and had control when things went bad. I believed that was enough.

I found out how wrong I was when I sat in that supervisor's seat. It was humbling to realize how much I did not know. The expectations shifted immediately. I was not responsible for myself anymore; I was responsible for everyone else on the shift, at the scene, and even more. Every decision carried more weight, which meant every hesitation mattered more. For the first time, I felt the pressure of knowing that what I said or did not say could directly impact someone else's outcome.

The Illusion I Had to Confront

The chair gave me authority the second I took it. What it most definitely did not give me was leadership. That realization hit hard. Because I had earned the position, I had not been forced to prove that I could lead under a completely different kind of pressure.

I could know policy and procedure and still hesitate or struggle to command a scene. I could hold rank and still feel the gap between being in charge and leading.

The Perspective Shift I Did not Expect

Sitting in that chair changed how I saw things, whether I wanted it to or not. I now had to start thinking about liability. I started considering how decisions would be reviewed later, not just how they would play out in the moment. I became more aware of the bigger picture, the administrative side, the things I did not have to think about before.

That shift is necessary. However, I also understand how it looks from the other side, because I have been there. I know what it feels like to watch a supervisor hesitate. I know how quickly that perception turns into something else. *"You have changed."* What that really means is simple and cuts deep: my coworkers, now my subordinates, do not feel I have led.

The Isolation I Was Not Prepared For

No one prepared me for how much things would change socially.

Conversations became different. The same people I used to talk to freely started holding back. Not out of disrespect, but because the dynamic had changed because I was not just one of them anymore.

However, I was not fully removed either; I was still not on the same level. That middle ground can get quiet if you let it. Leadership depends on understanding what your people are dealing with. If they stop talking, you lose that. If or when you lose that, you start making decisions without the full picture, and that is when mistakes happen.

When I Felt the Chair Start to Take Over

The most honest part of this is admitting that I have felt the shift.

It does not happen all at once. However, I started to notice things. I started leaning on policy for support more than judgment. I took an extra second before making decisions I would have made instantly before. Consequently, I started thinking about them in a way that slowed me down rather than sharpened my focus.

My shift noticed it before I did. They did not need to say it. I could feel it in how they responded. That is when I had to check myself.

Because if they are adapting around me, I am not leading the way I should be.

The Pressure Is Real

There is a part of this that does not get acknowledged enough. The pressure that comes with that rank is real.

Every decision has the potential to be reviewed, questioned, or criticized. You are expected to be right, often with limited information and no time. The margin for error feels like it disappears. That kind of pressure can make anyone hesitate.

Not because they are weak but because they understand what is at stake. Nevertheless, I have learned that hesitation carries its own consequences. In this job, things move fast. Officers need directions in real time. They do not need perfect decisions, but they need clear ones. That responsibility does not go away because the pressure increases.

What I have Learned About the Chair

The biggest lesson I have taken from sitting in that chair is this:

It does not change who I am, but it reveals who I am under pressure. If I relied too much on structure instead of thinking, it would show. If I had never developed real leadership before promotion, it would show. Likewise, if I were already leading before I ever got the promotion, that would show too.

The chair does not create leaders or mold them. But it does expose them.

The Truth I Carry with Me

I still sometimes hear the phrase "You have changed," and every time I hear it, it is taken as a reminder. Not of what happens to other people, but what can happen to me if I am not paying attention.

The chair is not magic; it never was and never will be.

The only question is whether I control it, or whether it controls me.

Chapter 9: The Danger of "We've Always Done It This Way"

There is a phrase in law enforcement that does more damage than anyone realizes. It does not sound aggressive or even wrong. In fact, it sounds somewhat reasonable.

"We have always done it this way." Alternatively, *"That is how it has been done."*

It is usually said with confidence and with some pride. However, what it represents is resistance: resistance to change, resistance to adaptation, and just plain resistance.

Where It Comes From

Tradition has value. Our profession, like many others, is built on experience, sacrifices, hard lessons, and practices that once worked. It is a core value, and it matters.

However, tradition can become a problem when it stops being questioned. When the ideology of tradition shifts from: "This works." To: "This is how it is done." Those are not the same thing.

When Experience Turns into Resistance

I learned that early on, when I lateraled to Georgia, I knew I was starting fresh—a new agency, a new environment, and new expectations. That did not bother me. What stood out was how ideas were received. I proposed changes—small ones at first, adjustments that made sense based on what I had seen work elsewhere.

To my surprise, some were accepted and even implemented. So, I pushed further. When a detective position opened, I applied. I had the experience and the work to back it up. I expected at least a conversation. There was not one. The position went to someone else. No explanation. Later, another position opened. Same process, same outcome.

When I asked why, the answer was not hidden behind policy or performance metrics. It was simple: "That is just how it has always been done." It was also commonly said that my experience helped me get hired. It did not mean my experience would be considered within the agency.

What That Actually Means

It means the system is protected and not evaluated. Tradition, when unchallenged, acts as a shield, blocking evaluation, avoiding accountability, and eliminating the need to justify decisions.

The Cost of That Mindset

Policing today is not the same as it was ten years ago. Nevertheless, in many areas, leadership has not kept pace. Policies stay the same because they are familiar. Training remains unchanged because it is comfortable. Supervision stays static because it is expected. The result is an organization that appears stable—but is quietly falling behind.

What the Line Sees

We noticed it first. We observe outdated methods being used to address modern issues. We see the disconnect between what leadership claims they will do and what is done, forgetting that actions speak louder than words.

Over time, that disconnect influences behavior. Not immediately, but gradually. Those of us who were proactive become reactive. Those of us who were once motivated, hard-charging officers have become cautious and reserved. Not because we lack the ability, but because the system does not support it.

The False Choice

Leadership often treats this as a choice: tradition or progress. That is the wrong approach. The real difference lies between principles and practices. Principles—such as *integrity, accountability, discipline*—remain constant. Practices must adapt because the environment changes. Holding onto outdated practices in the name of tradition does not strengthen the profession; it weakens it.

What Leadership Requires

Leadership in modern policing demands a willingness to challenge traditional systems. Not to dismantle them indiscriminately, but to assess systems such as policies and procedures. It involves questioning whether they still serve their purpose compared to what is operational. However, it also means being ready to change them when they do not, and that can be challenging.

It requires the ability to:

• Challenging established norms

• Accepting criticism

• Taking responsibility for change

But that is the job.

Tradition vs. Progress: A False Choice

It is crucial to be clear — tradition itself is not the problem. In fact, some of the most valuable aspects of policing are rooted in tradition: discipline, accountability, camaraderie, and a strong sense of duty.

The issue arises when tradition is seen as untouchable and unchangeable. Effective leadership understands the difference between principles and practices. Principles—such as integrity, service, and professionalism—should remain constant and act as guides for police officers. Practices—how those principles are enacted—must adapt over time.

For example, mentorship has long been a core part of policing. Traditionally, it was informal and learned through experience and observation. In modern policing, mentorship needs to be intentional, structured, and aligned with current challenges. The principle stays the same, but the methods change. Leaders who overlook this distinction often oppose needed change by hiding behind the idea of protecting tradition. In doing so, outdated practices are defended while (I hope) unintentionally weakening the very principles they are meant to uphold.

Reality

"We have always done it this way" is not a justification. It's a warning. Because once that mindset takes hold, improvement stops. Moreover, when improvement in a field that depends on adaptation stops, failure is not immediate. But it is unavoidable.

When leaders rely too heavily on tradition, they unintentionally create environments that block growth. We are expected to adapt to change, but leadership remains inflexible. This imbalance leads to frustration, dissent, and a "why bother?" mindset.

If leadership does not adapt, we lack relevant guidance. Without relevant guidance, we often fill the gap on our own. Some of us will adapt and succeed despite the system, but many will not, and an increasing number will leave an exodus that is already happening. This is not a failure of the individual; it is a failure of leadership to recognize that the profession has changed and to be willing to change with it.

Chapter 10: Institutional Ego

There is a big problem in law enforcement that rarely gets recognized. It does not show up in policies, it is not covered in training, and leaders rarely acknowledge it. However, it influences decisions more than any written rule—institutional ego.

What It Is & What It Is Not

Institutional ego is not confidence. It is not a commanding presence. It is not pride in the profession. It is the belief—spoken or unspoken—that:

• Rank equals correctness

• Authority overrides input

• Experience cannot be questioned

• Ideas are judged by source, not merit

It is when leadership stops asking, "What is the best solution?" and starts asking, "Who suggested it?" that the outcome is already decided.

How It Shows Up in Real Time

It rarely announces itself, but it appears in patterns. An officer proposes a practical solution, and it works. It solves a known problem but is dismissed—not because it is wrong, but because it did not come from the right source. Likewise, a supervisor finds a more effective way to allocate resources. It boosts efficiency and cuts risk. It gets delayed, reviewed, rewritten, and eventually buried. Not because it does not work, but because it disrupts the current structure. A command decision is obviously ineffective, and everyone recognizes it. No one changes it because doing so would require admitting failure. That is institutional ego.

What It Protects

It safeguards one's position within the agency. It protects personal image, especially if rank is tied to that image. It maintains authority, whether official or position-based. However, it does not protect the mission.

The Cost

When ego drives decision-making:

- Problems are managed instead of solved

- Feedback is filtered instead of heard

- Innovation slows

- Mistakes are hidden

What Officers Learn

We adapt quickly, and we learn:

- Who listens
- Who doesn't
- What ideas matter
- Whose ideas matter

When ideas are judged by rank rather than merit, performance declines and trust erodes. We stop speaking, not because we lack ideas, but because we know those ideas will not matter or be supported.

The Blind Spot

The most dangerous part of institutional ego is this: it does not feel like ego.

It appears as:

• Upholding standards

• Defending the organization

• Ensuring consistency

These are valid responsibilities. However, when used to avoid accountability or dismiss input, it ceases to be leadership. It becomes a barrier, and ego-driven leaders defend systems—even when those systems are failing.

The Self-Awareness Test

Every leader should be able to answer one question:

Do people bring their problems to you—or avoid you?

If they bring them:

- They trust you

- They expect action

- They believe you will listen

If they avoid you:

- They expect dismissal

- They anticipate resistance

- They have already adapted to you

That answer defines you as a leader.

What Real Leadership Looks Like Instead

Leadership without ego is not passive but disciplined.

It requires the ability to:

- Accept input without defensiveness

- Change direction without feeling exposed

- Admit mistakes without losing authority

- Evaluate ideas without attaching rank to them

Leadership without ego is not about weakness. It is about discipline. It is an honorable action, and it is not easy. In fact, it is one of the hardest transitions for leaders to make because it requires letting go of perceived strength.

Reality

Institutional ego will always be present. The real question is whether leadership lets it influence decisions or if they control them. Because when ego drives leadership:

- Innovation stops

- Trust erodes

- Performance declines

- Retention suffers

Moreover, the organization shifts from improving itself…to protecting itself.

Final Truth

Obviously, officers do not use the term "institutional ego."

We don't need to. We say:

- "They [command] do not listen."

- "It does not matter what we say."

- "They are [command] going to do what they want anyway."

- "They [command] already know whom they want for that spot."

That is the operational definition, and once that belief takes hold, leadership has already lost influence—regardless of rank. Because leadership is not about being right but about being effective, the moment ego outweighs effectiveness, leadership becomes the problem.

PART IV: CONSEQUENCES & LIABILITY

Chapter 11: Leadership Liability — When Rank Becomes Risk

Leadership in law enforcement is often discussed in terms of effectiveness, but it should also be examined in terms of liability. When leadership fails at the operational level, the consequences go beyond poor performance—they create risk. Not just abstract or theoretical risk, but real, measurable liability. Leadership liability cannot be solved with policy. It must be addressed through how leaders are selected, trained, and held accountable.

Defining Leadership Liability

Leadership liability occurs when a person in a position of authority becomes a source of risk instead of control. It is not simply ineffective leadership. It is leadership that:

- Fails to establish command

- Delays critical decision-making

- Creates confusion instead of clarity

- Avoids ownership during active incidents

At that point, rank is no longer stabilizing the situation. It is contributing to its deterioration.

Command vs Presence

Being present on the scene is not the same as being in command.

Command requires three things:

1. **Scene Ownership**

   Someone is clearly in charge. No ambiguity. No overlap.

2. **Role Assignment**

   Units are directed, not self-deploying.

3. **Operational Intent**

   Everyone understands the objective—not just their individual task.

When those elements are missing, what replaces them is predictable:

- Independent decision-making

- Redundant actions

- Gaps in coverage

- Delayed response

From the outside, it may still look functional. From the inside, it is fragmented.

ICS in Practice — Not Theory

Incident Command System principles exist for a purpose. Not for paperwork or compliance, but for control. At its core, ICS answers one question:

Who is in charge, and what is the plan?

When that answer is not clear, liability begins immediately.

It is seen in:

- Multiple units giving conflicting directions

- No defined perimeter or containment

- Failure to establish staging

- Lack of communication structure

These are not minor issues but are indicators of command failure.

The Three Points Where Liability Forms

Leadership liability consistently develops in three operational moments:

1. Initial Response

This is where control is either established or lost.

Key failures:

- No clear assumption of command

- Delayed scene assessment

- Units acting without coordination

Tactically, this results in:

- Missed threats

- Poor positioning

- Lack of situational awareness

Legally, this becomes:

- Failure to supervise

- Failure to control the scene

2. Escalation Phase

This is where hesitation becomes dangerous.

Conditions change. Information updates. Risk increases.

Key failures:

- Delayed decision-making

- Over-reliance on additional resources instead of action

- Waiting for perfect information

Tactically:

- Time is lost

- Opportunities are missed

- Conditions worsen

From a command perspective, this is the point where *Inaction becomes a decision.*

3. Post-Incident Accountability

This is where leadership either reinforces trust—or destroys it.

Key failures:

- Lack of ownership

- Public or internal second-guessing without context

- Failure to support reasonable decisions

This does not just affect morale. It directly impacts future performance. Officers start adjusting their behavior based on expected reactions—not on operational necessity. That shift introduces long-term organizational risk.

What Courts and Reviews Actually Look At

In any major incident, review bodies do not ask:

"Was someone present?"

They ask:

- Who was in command?

- Were roles clearly assigned?

- Was there a coordinated plan?

- Were decisions made in a reasonable timeframe?

Those answers determine:

- Civil liability

- Administrative findings

- Organizational accountability

Leadership is evaluated through action—not intent.

Operational Reality

Leadership liability is rarely recognized in the moment, but it is always visible afterward—on body camera, in radio traffic, on timelines, and in reports. Every hesitation, lack of direction, and moment of confusion is documented and reviewed.

The Critical Failure

The most dangerous leadership failure is not making the wrong decision. It is failing to make one.

Because in dynamic situations:

- Delay increases risk

- Confusion creates gaps

- Lack of direction forces independent action

Once officers begin operating independently, command is already compromised.

The Standard That Matters

Effective command is not about perfection. It's about control.

- Clear direction

- Timely decisions

- Ownership of outcomes

That is what stabilizes a scene. That is what reduces risk. That is what protects both officers and the organization.

The Bottom Line

Leadership is not just about performance. It is about responsibility, and when leadership fails operationally, the cost is not measured in criticism.

It is measured in:

- Officer safety

- Public safety

- Legal exposure

- Organizational credibility

At that point, rank is no longer an asset but a liability.

Chapter 12: Case Study -Command Failure in Real Time (Uvalde)

I approached Uvalde the same way I approach any chaotic scene. I watch, listen, and identify control. Then ask one question: *Who is in charge?* Because everything that follows depends on that answer.

The First Minutes

May 24, 2022, in Uvalde, Texas. The call comes in: active shooter at an elementary school.

Officers respond immediately with no delay. There is no staging in the area waiting. *Immediate response.*

Within minutes, units are on scene, and additional agencies begin to arrive. Patrol, supervisors, specialized units. Equipment is there, training is there, personnel are there. Everything that should matter is present. From the outside, it looks like a functioning response. From the inside, something is already off.

Initial Contact

Officers enter the school and move toward the threat. Gunfire is exchanged. At that moment, the situation is clearly defined.

Active shooter.

Doctrine is not unclear here. It has been reinforced for decades:

- Move to the threat

- Stop the killing

- Neutralize immediately

(Advanced Law Enforcement Rapid Response Training [ALERRT], 2020)

There is no delay built into that model. There is no pause for perfect coordination. Action is the one and only expectation. For a moment, that response begins, then something changes.

Critical Misidentification

The suspect retreats into a classroom, and somewhere in that transition, the problem is redefined.

Not clearly announced and not formally communicated across all units. But operationally, everything shifts. The situation begins to be treated as a *barricaded subject*. That single shift changes the entire response. Why?

Because:

- An active shooter requires immediate action

- A barricaded subject allows time

One creates urgency while the other creates hesitation. Subsequent investigations confirmed this misclassification as a central failure point (Texas House of Representatives, 2022; U.S. Department of Justice, 2024).

Time Begins to Stretch

Minutes pass. Officers are *inside* the building. Not outside or waiting on the perimeter, but inside.

Positioned in the hallway with weapons ready. More officers arrive, and the hallway fills with personnel. Resources continue to stack and stack. From the inside, control is missing. There's no clearly established incident commander; no unified operational plan communicated across agencies. Radio traffic reflects it, with questions asked without answers. Updates given without coordination and information without action.

Presence Without Command

There was no shortage of personnel, no shortage of rank, but there was a shortage of command.

Command answers three things immediately:

- Who is in charge

- What is the objective

- Who is responsible for what

When those answers are unclear, operations do not stop, but they fragment. Officers begin operating based on individual interpretation. Small groups form where decisions are made locally, not collectively. No one is deliberately doing the wrong thing, but no one is clearly directing the right one.

The Hallway

Time continues to pass, ten minutes, twenty minutes, thirty minutes. Officers are still holding in position while the threat remains active. This is where leadership matters. Not from the policy manual or the last training session. Right there in that hallway at that moment. Where the decision is simple, but the consequences are not. Move forward and accept risk or wait and accept a different risk.

The Cost of Hesitation

As time passes, the environment changes. Not physically but operationally. There's a shift from action to waiting. From clarity to uncertainty. From what started as a movement to hesitation. This is what leadership failure looks like in real time.

Controlled inaction.

Once the situation was misidentified, hesitation became justifiable, and delay became explainable. From there, waiting became defensible even though none of that changed reality. That reality was that the victims were still inside.

Investigations later confirmed that victims remained alive during portions of the delay (U.S. Department of Justice, 2024). That is the operational consequence of misidentified leadership intent.

Command Breakdown Timeline (Operational View)

Phase 1: Initial Response (0–5 Minutes)

- Officers arrive rapidly

- Entry is made

- Gunfire exchanged

- **Correct classification: Active shooter**

Leadership Standard: Immediate aggressive engagement

Reality: Initial movement aligns with training

Phase 2: Transition Point (5–15 Minutes)

- Suspect enters classroom

- Situation informally reclassified

- No unified command established

Failure Point:

- Misidentification of incident type

- No clearly communicated command authority

(Texas House of Representatives, 2022)

Phase 3: Containment Without Command (15–45 Minutes)

- Officers remain in hallway

- Additional units stack

- No coordinated breach initiated

Operational Indicators:

- Conflicting information

- No clear objective

- Decentralized decision-making

Leadership Failure:

- No scene ownership

- No decisive action

(U.S. Department of Justice, 2024)

Phase 4: Prolonged Delay (45–77 Minutes)

- Resources remain available

- Victims still inside

- No unified operational push

Critical Issue:

- Inaction becomes normalized

- Responsibility diffuses across agencies

(ALERRT, 2020; DOJ, 2024)

Phase 5: Final Resolution (~77 Minutes)

- Breach conducted

- Suspect neutralized

Outcome Reality:

- Resolution occurs despite earlier delay

- Opportunity for earlier intervention lost

What Failed

This was not a failure of training, equipment, staffing, or even the response time. All of that was present. What failed was leadership.

Specifically, the problem was not correctly defined; there was no establishment of command or the intent of command; and there was a complete failure to act decisively under pressure.

Once the problem was misidentified, everything that followed aligned with that error. Why? Because leadership sets direction, and that direction guides performance.

The Lesson That Cannot Be Ignored

Leadership is not tested when things go right but exposed when things go wrong.

Furthermore, in those moments, there is no time for perfect information. There is also no time to reach a consensus or ensure alignment with policy. The only responsibility is: *Take control. Define the problem and act.*

The Hard Question

Every officer who studies this incident will ask themselves, "What would I have done?"

That is not the right question to ask. The right question is "*If I were in charge, would I have taken control?*" That is where leadership exists, in the moment where hesitation competes with responsibility, not in hindsight and not in reports.

Final Reality

Uvalde is not difficult to understand. That is what makes it difficult to accept. There is no complex solution to review, and no new high-tech system to implement. Everything was there: rank, personnel, resources, opportunity. The only shortage was leadership.

Final Line

In the end, the question was never who was there. The question was: *who was in command?*

Furthermore, when that answer is not clear, everything else fails.

Chapter 13: The Constants of Command- A Leadership Blueprint

Leadership in law enforcement does not need to be reinvented. It needs to be applied consistently. Across agencies, across assignments, across conditions, the same traits appear in leaders who are trusted, followed, and effective under pressure. They are not complicated, and they are not optional.

1. Presence — The Foundation of Command

Presence is not physical location. It is engagement. A supervisor can be absent and still be present.

Presence means:

- Actively assessing the situation

- Communicating with purpose

- Positioning yourself where decisions are made—not observed

From the line, presence is immediately recognized by officers. We know when someone is engaged and when they are not. That determines how the rest of the scene develops. Because when leadership is present, hesitation decreases. When it is not, it spreads.

2. Clarity — Direction Without Confusion

Clarity eliminates hesitation. In dynamic situations, clarity matters more than perfection. Officers do not need complete information, but direction.

Clarity looks like:

- Defined objectives

- Simple, direct communication

- Prioritized actions

It removes hesitation, and it aligns movement. It allows people to act without waiting for constant instruction. Without clarity, even experienced officers begin to slow down—not from lack of ability, but from lack of direction.

3. Decisiveness — Action Under Uncertainty

Leadership requires decisions to be made. Every call involves incomplete information. Waiting for certainty is not a strategy; it is avoidance. Decisiveness is not about being right every time but about making a reasonable decision within a reasonable timeframe. That decision can be adjusted, but delay cannot be recovered.

From a command perspective:

- Action creates options

- Inaction removes them

That distinction defines outcomes.

4. Accountability — Ownership Without Deflection

Accountability is where leadership either solidifies—or collapses.

It applies in two directions:

Downward:

- Supporting reasonable decisions

- Correcting without humiliation

- Taking responsibility for team outcomes

Upward:

- Owning decisions

- Accepting consequences

- Avoiding blame-shifting

When accountability is consistent, trust builds. When it is selective, trust disappears.

5. Consistency

Trust is built continuously and through repetition, not just through intensity. Officers track patterns of behavior. The most effective leaders do not micromanage every action. They communicate with their intent, allowing officers to adapt when conditions change.

Instead of saying: "Do exactly this." It becomes: "This is what we are trying to accomplish."

The Standard

These are not personality traits. These are much-needed expectations of behavior. Presence, clarity, decisiveness, accountability, and intent. When these qualities are present, performance improves—not because the job becomes easier, but because leadership becomes effective and repeatable.

Chapter 14: Cultural Reform— Changing What Actually Drives Behavior

Culture is not defined by policy but shaped by behavior. What is rewarded, what is tolerated, and what is ignored. This is what shapes an organization.

The Reality of Culture

All agencies and organizations say they value initiative, leadership, and critical thinking. However, their actions show that they reward compliance, silence, and risk avoidance. That massive contradiction defines culture.

Where Culture Breaks

Culture breaks when there is a disconnect between what is said, what is enforced, and what is practiced. The concept is simple: *say what you mean and mean what you say*. Officers recognize that disconnect immediately, and once we do, we stop listening to what is said and respond to what is reinforced.

What Drives Behavior

Three things shape behavior: *is there a reward, are there consequences, and what is observed?*

The operating standard is set after noting those three things. We learn quickly: *what gets recognized, what gets ignored, and what gets punished.* Regardless of what policy dictated, the actions taken and observed spoke louder than the words.

What Needs to Change

Cultural reform does not require large-scale restructuring.

It requires consistency in specific areas:

1. Redefining What Is Rewarded

If agencies continue to reward:

- Compliance with decision-making

- Silence over input

- Risk avoidance over problem-solving

That is the same result they will get.

If the agencies redefine their leadership styles and reward:

- Initiative

- Sound judgment

- Ownership

The behavior of every subordinate will change. Not immediately—but predictably and exponentially.

2. Supporting Decision-Making

As officers, it is imperative to us that we understand that if we make a reasonable decision, we will be supported and not face that decision alone. Without that support, decision-making slows down and hesitation increases risk.

3. Eliminating Institutional Ego

Ideas must be evaluated on merit—not source. That is going to require leaders to be willing to change and be a part of a system that allows input without penalty. It also means recognition of good ideas and that the ideas were not rank-dependent. If that can be done, engagement will increase. Conversely, if it cannot be done, silence will take over.

4. Aligning Words with Action

If leadership says:

"We support initiative." However, punishes it when it creates friction—The message is clear, and it is not the one intended. Consistency matters more than messaging.

The Role of Leadership in Culture

Leadership does not merely observe culture. It actively creates it. Every decision reinforces value. Every response establishes a standard. Every action becomes part of the pattern officers follow.

The Reality Leaders Must Accept

Officers will always adapt. However, the question is what are they adapting to? *The mission, or the system protecting itself?* That answer will determine the effectiveness of the organization's leadership.

The main point to remember.

Cultural reform is not about changing perception but changing behavior. Behavior will change when expectations are clear, decisions are supported, and leadership is consistent.

Without that, nothing else matters.

Conclusion

There is no shortage of policies in law enforcement. There is no shortage of training or structure. What is missing in too many places is leadership—not in title, but in function.

The gap between rank and leadership is not subtle, but it is visible. It appears in scenes where no one steps up to take control, in decisions that are delayed rather than made, and in officers who stop expecting direction—and start relying on each other instead.

The system does not fail immediately; it adapts. Workarounds develop, informal leaders emerge, and the job still gets done. However, not as originally designed. Over time, that has serious consequences that an agency will struggle to get ahead of. Morale will decline, retention will suffer, and performance will drop.

Not because officers are incapable. Because leadership is inconsistent, remember that all that is being requested is Presence, Clarity, and Accountability. That is it. No theories, no speeches, no positions. Just function.

Chapter 15: Stepping Off the Soapbox

At some point, every conversation about leadership reaches a limit.

You can define it. Break it down and analyze it. You can write policies around it. Test for it and endlessly talk about it. However, eventually, all of that must stop. Because leadership is not something you explain but something you do.

Everything in this book comes back to one reality: Leadership is a behavior. It is not a rank or a position. It is not in a title but in one's behavior. You do not become a leader when you get promoted. You become a leader the moment people look to you—and you decide what to do next.

That moment does not come with a warning. It does not come when everything is controlled. It arrives when information is incomplete, conditions are unstable, and someone must take responsibility. That is the moment this entire book is about. Not the classroom theory. Not the agency's structure or the process. The moment.

Because when that moment arrives, there are only two outcomes: You take control, or you do not. Moreover, if you do not, someone else will. Not because they are assigned to do so, but because the situation demands it. That is the reality most organizations avoid. There are always two chains of command: the one on paper and the one that actually operates under pressure.

Rank Isn't Leadership

On paper, authority is based on rank, but real influence comes from trust. You do not decide who people follow; the subordinates do. They decide based on what they have observed, what you have done, and whether you have shown up when it mattered.

That is how leadership is evaluated. Not annually, not formally, but constantly. This profession does not fail because people cannot do the job. It fails when leadership does not match responsibility. When rank is present—but leadership is not.

Furthermore, when that happens, people adapt. They stop expecting direction, and they rely on each other.

They work around the system instead of within it. That adaptation keeps things functioning.

But it comes at a cost. Trust erodes, initiative declines, performance drops from optimal levels to minimal, and eventually, people leave. That is not a staffing issue or a training problem. That is a leadership issue. The solution isn't complicated or new. It's not even theoretical.

Leadership requires presence when it matters, clarity when things are unclear, decisiveness when information is incomplete, and accountability when outcomes are imperfect. That's it. Does not mean it is easy. But it is simple.

Moreover, the standard does not change based on rank; if anything, it increases. Because the higher you go, the more people depend on your decisions. At some point, you must step off the soapbox. Stop explaining leadership. Stop defining it. Stop expecting it to come from somewhere else and start acting.

Because when the next call comes in, and it will, no one is going to ask: "What does policy say?" "What does training recommend?" "What should we do in theory?" They are going to look for one thing: Who is in charge.

Moreover, more importantly, *are they leading?*

That is where this book ends, not with an answer, but with entrusted responsibility. Because the gap between rank and leadership does not close on its own, it closes when someone chooses in that moment to step forward and take control. Furthermore, when that happens, everything changes.

References

Burrows, D. (2022). *Investigative Committee on the Robb Elementary Shooting.* Austin: Texas House of Representatives.

Dr. Joseph J. Lestrange, C. J. (2024, October 21). *Police1.* Retrieved from Police1: https://www.police1.com/chiefs-sheriffs/the-battle-against-misinformation-and-disinformation-campaigns-is-your-police-department-prepared

Hayward, S. F. (n.d.). *Churchill on Leadership : Executive Success in the Face of Adversity.* 1998: PRH Christian Publishing.

Hope, K. R. (2020). Civilian Oversight for Democratic Policing and its Challenges: Overcoming Obstacles for Improved Police Accountability. *Journal of Applied Security Research.*

Mattis, J., & West, B. (2019). *Call Sign Chaos.* Random House.

Ph.D, K. M. (2002). *Emotional survival for law enforcement: A guide for officers and their families.* E-S Press.

Phillips, D. (1992). *Lincoln on Leaderhsip.* Warner Books, Inc.

Police Executive Research Forum. (2023, April 1). *Police Executive Research Forum*. Retrieved from Police Forum: https://perf.memberclicks.net/

Strock, J. (2003). *Theodore Roosevelt on Leadership: Executive Lessons from the Bully Pulpit.* Forum Books.

USAF, M. M. (2015). *The Chesty Puller Paragon: Leadership Dogma Or Model Doctrine?* Lucknow Books.

Wynn, M. (2008). *Rising Through the Ranks.* Kaplan Publishing.

Advanced Law Enforcement Rapid Response Training (ALERRT). (2020). *Active shooter response guidelines.* Texas State University.

Texas House of Representatives. (2022). *Investigative committee report on the Robb Elementary shooting.*

U.S. Department of Justice. (2024). *Critical incident review: Uvalde, Texas.* Office of Community Oriented Policing Services.

9 798904 173654